## Program Authors

Peter Afflerbach

Camille Blachowicz

Candy Dawson Boyd

Wendy Cheyney

Connie Juel

Edward Kame'enui

Donald Leu

Jeanne Paratore

P. David Pearson

Sam Sebesta

Deborah Simmons

Sharon Vaughn

Susan Watts-Taffe

Karen Kring Wixson

**PEARSON**

Scott
Foresman

**Editorial Offices:** Glenview, Illinois • Parsippany, New Jersey • New York, New York
**Sales Offices:** Needham, Massachusetts • Duluth, Georgia • Glenview, Illinois
Coppell, Texas • Sacramento, California • Mesa, Arizona

We dedicate Reading Street to
Peter Jovanovich.

His wisdom, courage,
and passion for education
are an inspiration to us all.

## About the Cover Artist

Daniel Moreton lives in New York City, where he uses his computer to create illustrations for books. When he is not working, Daniel enjoys cooking, watching movies, and traveling. On a trip to Mexico, Daniel was inspired by all of the bright colors around him. He likes to use those colors in his art.

ISBN: 0-328-10829-4

Copyright © 2007 Pearson Education, Inc.

4 5 6 7 8 9 10 V063 14 13 12 11 10 09 08 07 06

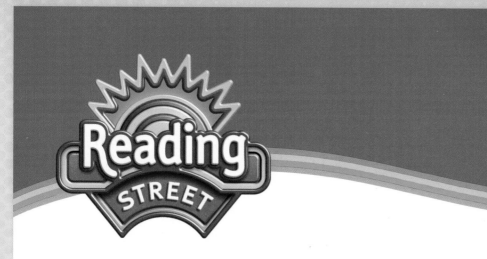

Dear Reader,

Are you enjoying your travels along *Scott Foresman Reading Street?* What new skills have you learned to help you read and understand new things? What strategies have helped you smooth out the "bumps in the road" as you read?

As you continue along *Scott Foresman Reading Street,* you will read about people in communities at home, in school, and in neighborhoods. You will also read about communities in nature. So, buckle your seat belt and enjoy the trip!

Sincerely,
The Authors

## What is a community?

## People in Communities

# Communities in Nature

# UNIT
# 2

# Communities

## What is a community?

# Max and Ruby:
# A Big Fish for Max

## A rabbit family has fun together.

**ANIMAL FANTASY**

connect to SOCIAL STUDIES

# The Farmer
# in the Hat

## Students work together in school.

**REALISTIC FICTION**

connect to SOCIAL STUDIES

# Who Works Here?

## Many people work in a community.

**EXPOSITORY NONFICTION**

connect to SOCIAL STUDIES

# The Big Circle

## Animals work together to keep one another safe.

**FICTION**

connect to SCIENCE

# Life in the Forest

## Plants and animals live together in a forest.

**EXPOSITORY NONFICTION**

connect to SCIENCE

# Honey Bees

## Bees are insects that live in communities.

**EXPOSITORY NONFICTION**

connect to SCIENCE

# Let's Talk About

# People in Communities

# Words to Read

| |
|---|
| **want** |
| **good** |
| **catch** |
| **no** |
| **put** |

## Read the Words

**1.** Max said, "I want a fish."

**2.** Fish are good to eat.

**3.** Will Max catch a fish?

**4.** No fish bit.

**5.** We put the fish in a pan.

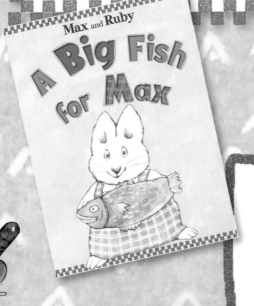

**Genre: Animal Fantasy**
An animal fantasy is a story with animals that act like humans. Next you will read about Max and Ruby—rabbits that go fishing.

## Max and Ruby

# A Big Fish for Max

written and designed by

## Rosemary Wells

illustrated

## by Jody Wheeler

Where will Max
get a big fish?

"I wish I had a fish to eat," said Max.

"Then we will catch a big fish,"
said Grandma.

"We can walk to the park," said Ruby.

"And Max will catch a big fish."

"Good," said Max. "Yum, yum, yum!"

The path in the park led to the pond.

"Max can fish in this pond," said Ruby.

Max sat.

He got a red ball in his net.

But no fish bit.

Then Max got a black ship in his net.
But no fish bit.

And then Max got a clam shell
in his net.

"I want to call the fish," said Ruby.
"Then I can talk to the fish."
But still no fish bit.

"Well, we can all walk to the fish
shop," said Grandma.
"And we can talk to the fish man."

The fish man had lots of fish in a box.
"We want a fresh fish," said Grandma.
"That fat fish is good."

At home, Grandma put the fish
in a hot pan.
Then Ruby put the fish in a dish.

"Yum, yum, yum!" said Max.

# Think and Share

**Talk About It** Max, Ruby, and Grandma care about each other. Find and read one part of the story that shows caring.

**1.** Use the pictures below to retell the story.

**2.** What was this story mostly about?

**3.** As you read, did you predict that Max would catch a fish? Find the part of the story that shows whether you were right.

**Look Back and Write** Look back at pages 20–22. Max did not catch a fish. What did he catch? Write those things.

## Meet the Author
# Rosemary Wells

Ms. Wells says, "Some of my most pleasurable memories as a child were of fishing with my father. We used to catch snapper blues, and my mother cooked them in parsley and butter that night. Today fish is still one of my favorite things to eat."

When Rosemary Wells writes stories about Max and Ruby, she thinks about what her own two girls said and did when they were children.

**Read other books by Rosemary Wells.**

# At Home

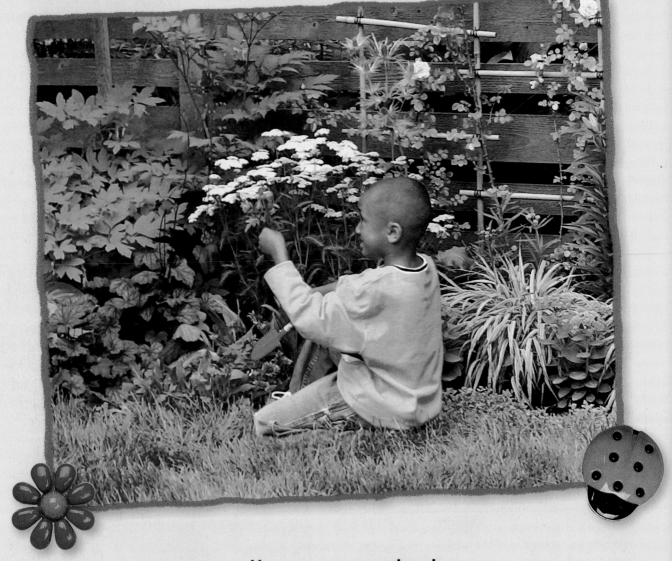

We all want to help.
This plant is no good.
We dig it up.

Dad puts pots on the shelf.

Mom cuts the grass.

Sis can catch Gus.
We talk and have fun.

# Nouns

• • • • • • • • • • • • • • • • • • • • • • • • • •

A **noun** names a person, a place, an animal, or a thing.

• • • • • • • • • • • • • • • • • • • • • • • • • •

The word **man** names a person.

The word **park** names a place.

The word **fish** names an animal.

The word **net** names a thing.

# Write Using Nouns

**1.** Write the three things Max got in his net. Their names are nouns.

. . . . . . . . . . . . . . . . . . . . . . . . . . . .

**2.** What place did Max, Ruby, and Grandma visit? Write a sentence about it. Draw a line under each noun.

. . . . . . . . . . . . . . . . . . . . . . . . . . . .

**3.** What did Max do to get a fish? Write the steps he took. Draw a line under each noun you use.

# Let's Talk About

## People in Communities

# Words to Read

| could |
|-------|
| be |
| old |
| paper |
| horse |

# Read the Words

1. Dave could be the pig in the class play.

2. Beth has an old hat for the play.

3. The class made paper masks.

4. Jake made a horse mask.

The Farmer in the Hat

**Genre: Realistic Fiction**
Realistic fiction has characters that act like real people. You will read a story about classmates putting on a play.

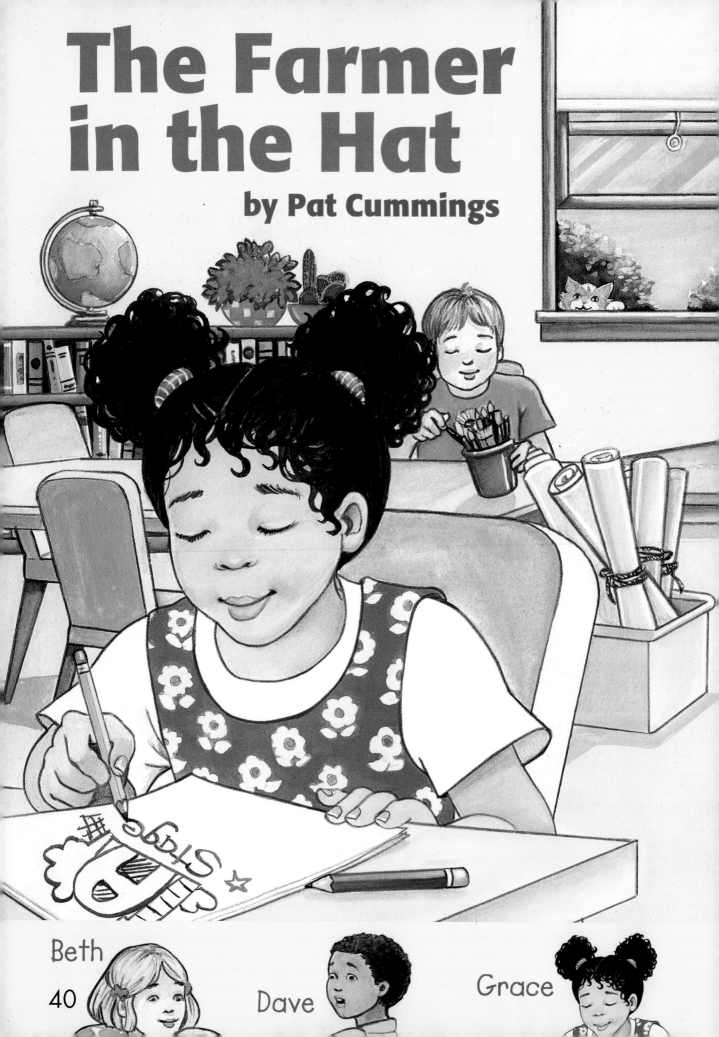

# The Farmer in the Hat

## by Pat Cummings

Beth

Dave

Grace

Who will be the farmer in the play?

Max

Jake

Meg

"I have the hat. I could be the farmer, Old MacDonald, in this play," said Beth.

"No, I will be the
farmer," said Dave.

"You can be a pig," said Beth.
"A pig!" Dave made a face.

Grace went up on the stage. "We could make paper masks," she said. "Ducks, hens, a pig, a horse!"

"I have the hat!" said Max.
"I will be Old MacDonald,
not Beth!"

"Let me have that hat!" Dave said.

"Stop!" said Grace. "We must make masks."

Old MacDonald
★ Hens = Beth and Grace
★ Pig = Dave
★ Duck = Max
★ Farmer = ?

47

Max made a duck on his page.
Beth made hens.

Dave made a pig mask on his page.

"That is one odd pig," Grace said.

"It takes ages to make this horse mask," said Jake.

"I can make my mask fast," said Meg.

She made a fat gerbil mask.

"Place that gerbil in a paper cage,"
Jake said with a grin.

"Take your places up on the stage," said Grace.

"Grunt!" Dave had on his pig mask.

"Squeak!" said Meg.

"Quack!" Max had on his duck mask.

"Cluck." Beth had on her hen mask.

"Look at the cat!" said Grace.
"That is one odd farmer!"

# Think and Share

**Talk About It** The author wrote a funny story about a class play. Read your favorite part of the story.

**1.** Use the pictures below to retell the story.

**2.** Why did the children forget about the farmer's hat?

**3.** The pictures give a clue about how the story will end. What clues do you see?

**Look Back and Write** Look back at the story. List the animals that will be in the play.

**Meet the Author and Illustrator**

# Pat Cummings

Pat Cummings once played a rabbit in a school play, and her sister played a grasshopper. Ms. Cummings made the cat the farmer in this story because "cats seem to naturally find the center of attention."

Ms. Cummings loves writing children's books. "The best part is that I can explore almost any subject."

**Read two more books by Pat Cummings.**

# Helping Hands at 4-H

by Lindy Russell

Where could you see what farmers do? At a 4-H club!

How old are kids in 4-H? They can be ages 8 to 18.

At 4-H you can take care of a horse or a pig.

You can get the eggs from the hens.

This 4-H club has a bake sale.
They place an ad in the paper.
They sell eggs too.

Bake Sale

Eggs
$ 2.00

The sale is good!
The club will get chicks.

The chicks will get big.
Then the club will have lots
of eggs to sell.

# Proper Nouns

Special names for people, places, animals, and things are called **proper nouns.** Proper nouns begin with capital letters.

**M**ax took the hat from **B**eth.

**M**ax and **B**eth are proper nouns. They tell the names of a girl and a boy. **M**ax and **B**eth begin with capital letters.

# Write Using Proper Nouns

**1.** Pick three children from the story. Their names are proper nouns. Write their names.

· · · · · · · · · · · · · · · · · · · · · · · · · · · · · · ·

**2.** Your name and your friend's name are proper nouns. Write a sentence using your name and a friend's name. Did you use capital letters?

· · · · · · · · · · · · · · · · · · · · · · · · · · · · · · ·

**3.** Could you make a mask for Old MacDonald? How would you do it? Write the steps. Use capital letters for proper nouns.

# Let's Talk About
# People in Communities

Mayor Sterling

Commonwealth
1800 N
Av

POLICE

# Words to Read

| |
|---|
| people |
| live |
| work |
| who |
| out |

# Read the Words

**1.** People live here.

**2.** People work here too.

**3.** Who works here?

**4.** Who puts out fires?

**Genre: Nonfiction**

Nonfiction tells about real people and events. Next you will read about real people who live and work in a neighborhood.

# Who Works

## Who works where you live?

# Here?

by Melissa Blackwell Burke
illustrated by Tim Spransy

People live and work
in this neighborhood.
It is such a busy place.

Who works in this place?
We will talk to them.
They all like to help us.

I make the neighborhood safe.
When you ride your bike,
stop and check all ways.
I will help you cross.

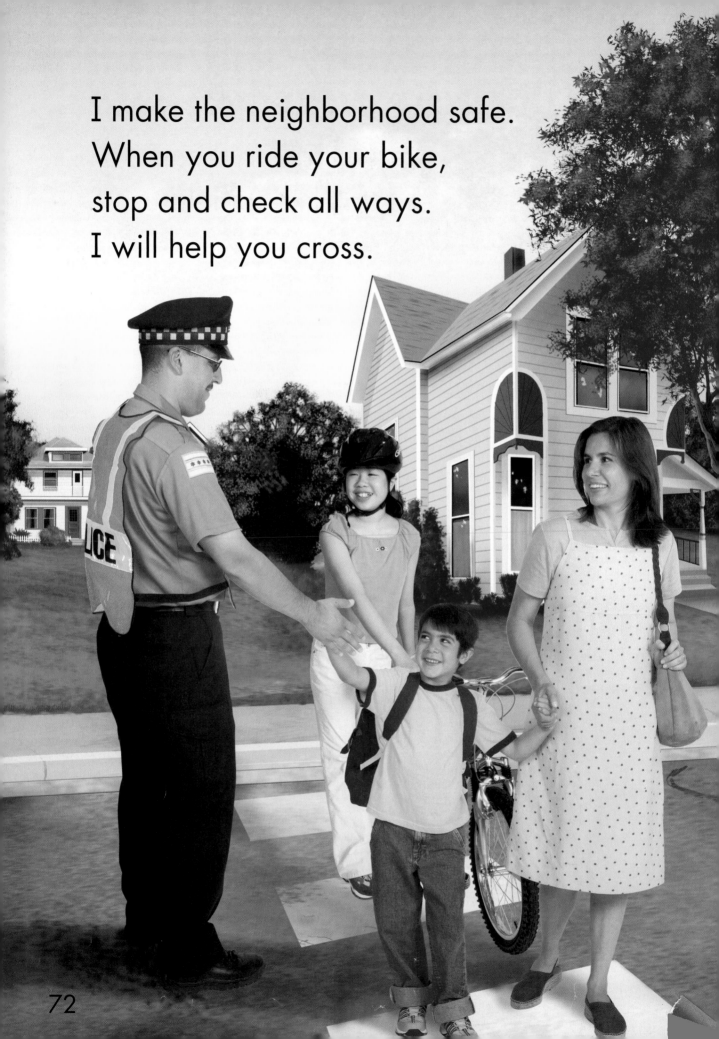

I help put out fires. Fire can be bad.
I wish all people could be safe
from fire.

I put mail in your box.
People stop and wave and smile.
They like to chat a while.

I drive a big bus.
People can ride this bus to work.
I stop and pick them up.

I pick up trash.
When people put it out,
I pitch it in this truck.

Who works where you live?
Smile at them.
You will like them!

# Think and Share

**Talk About It** *Who Works Here?* is about workers in a community. Tell about the job that interests you the most.

1. Use the pictures below to summarize what you learned.

2. What important information did the author want you to know?

3. Did anything confuse you? What question did you ask yourself as you read?

**Look Back and Write** Look back at page 77. What does this worker do?

# Melissa Blackwell Burke

Melissa Blackwell Burke grew up in a small town in Texas. She loved to visit the library. She says, "When I was a little girl, I wanted to be many things, including a teacher, a newspaper reporter, and a librarian. I have been two of those—a teacher and a newspaper reporter. Who knows—I might still become a librarian some day!"

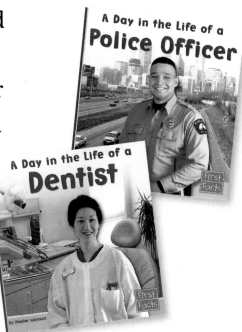

**Read other books about neighborhood workers.**

79

# Neighborhood Map

Use this map to check out where people live and work in this busy neighborhood.

- ⚙ Who works on Pine Lane?

- ⚙ Who works on Park Drive?

- ⚙ Where is the bus stop?

- ⚙ Where can you get stamps?

- ⚙ Where is the truck that picks up the trash?

## White Lane

Elm Drive

Park Drive

## Pine Lane

**Read Together**

# Special Titles

A **title** can come before the name of a person. A title begins with a capital letter. Some titles end with a **period(.)**.

**Officer** Black helps me cross the street.

**Ms.** Timms brings us letters.

**Dr.** Vann is a vet.

**Officer, Ms.,** and **Dr.** are special titles. Each begins with a capital letter. The titles **Ms.** and **Dr.** end with periods.

# Write Using Special Titles

**1.** Make up names for some of the workers in *Who Works Here?* Write their names using special titles with capital letters and periods.

**2.** Write a sentence about someone who works in your neighborhood. Use capital letters and periods for special titles.

**3.** How does your teacher start your school day? Write about it. Use capital letters and periods for special titles.

# Let's Talk About
# Communities
# in Nature

# Words to Read

| |
|---|
| there |
| down |
| inside |
| now |
| together |

# Read the Words

1. I smell a baby there.

2. T. Rex ran up the slope and down.

3. The small animals went inside the circle.

4. Now T. Rex couldn't get his lunch.

5. They like being together.

**Genre: Fiction**

Fiction stories are made-up stories. Next you will read a made-up story about dinosaurs that lived a long time ago.

# The Big Circle

by Eric Kimmel

illustrated by Richard Bernal

Who lived here long ago?

Big T. Rex wakes up.
Now Big T. Rex wants to eat,
but not bones and not stones.

Big T. Rex wants meat to eat.

Here is a herd of triceratops.
They are going home.

There they can get good grass to munch. The grass at home will make them fat.

Sniff, sniff. "Hmm," said Big T. Rex. "My nose smells a baby there. I'm good at hunting. I'll get that baby. It will make a good lunch."

Big T. Rex rose up on his back legs. He ran up the slope and down. The herd saw T. Rex run up and down.

They had time to make a big circle. The small animals went inside the circle. The baby went inside too.

Big T. Rex didn't like this.
Now he couldn't get his lunch.

But T. Rex didn't quit. "I'll make that herd run," he said.

But the herd didn't run.
They kept still in the big circle.

Then they gave T. Rex a poke and a bump. Together they drove him back.

Big T. Rex ran back up the slope and down. Those triceratops saw T. Rex run. Now they are safe.

They are going home to munch grass. Big T. Rex can't get them now. They like being together.

# Think and Share

**Talk About It** The author wrote an exciting story about dinosaurs. Which part of the story did you like best? Why?

**1.** Use the pictures below to retell the story.

**2.** What happened after the triceratops saw Big T. Rex?

**3.** As you read the story, did anything confuse you? What did you do?

**Look Back and Write** Look back at the selection. Write about how the triceratops protect the baby.

## Meet the Author and the Illustrator

# Eric Kimmel

As a boy Eric Kimmel visited the Museum of Natural History in New York City almost every weekend. "The dinosaur skeletons were old friends," he says. "Triceratops and stegosaurus were my favorites."

# Richard Bernal

Richard Bernal drew the pictures for this story. "I love dinosaurs," he says. "I have several dinosaur toys in my studio."

**Read other books by Eric Kimmel and Richard Bernal.**

# Class Paper

## Ms. Bell and Class Take Trip

## Big Bones

Ms. Bell and her class went on a trip. They saw bones from a T. Rex.

They saw bones from
a triceratops. There aren't
animals like this now.

# Cave Men

The class sat down and saw a film telling of cave men. Cave men went inside caves to live. They went hunting together.

Ms. Bell said, "I'm glad we went on this trip. We'll take many trips like this."

# Days, Months, and Holidays

**Days** of the week, **months** of the year, and **holidays** all begin with capital letters.

Big T. Rex woke up on **Saturday.**

The triceratops went home to munch grass in **March.**

**Mother's Day** is next **Sunday.**

# Write Using Days, Months, and Holidays

1. When is your birthday? Write the month. Look at a calendar. On what day of the week is your birthday this year? Write the day. Use capital letters.

· · · · · · · · · · · · · · · · · · · · · · · · · · ·

2. Write a sentence about your favorite month. Be sure to use capital letters correctly.

· · · · · · · · · · · · · · · · · · · · · · · · · · ·

3. What if there were a Dinosaur's Day? Tell two things you could do to celebrate this holiday.

# Let's Talk About
# Communities
# in Nature

# Words to Read

| grow |
| food |
| around |
| find |
| water |
| under |

# Read the Words

1. The sun helps plants and trees grow.

2. Plants are good food for insects.

3. Birds look around to find insects to eat.

4. Water makes logs damp.

5. Grubs live under rocks and logs.

Life in the Forest

**Genre: Expository Nonfiction**
Expository nonfiction tells facts about real places. Next you will read about the plants and animals in a forest.

# Life in the Forest

by Claire Daniel

# What lives in the forest?

We can find life all around the forest.
It is a busy place!

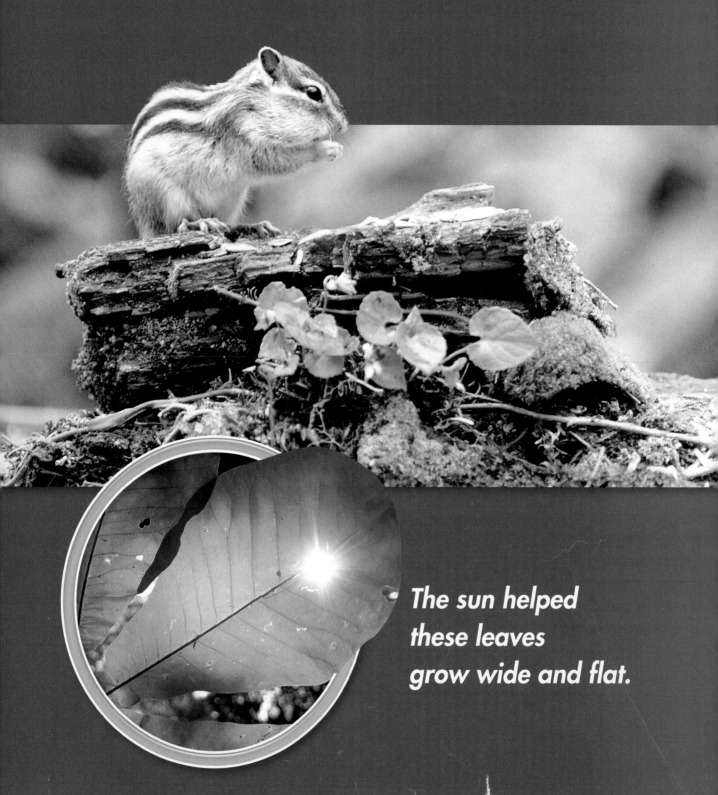

*The sun helped these leaves grow wide and flat.*

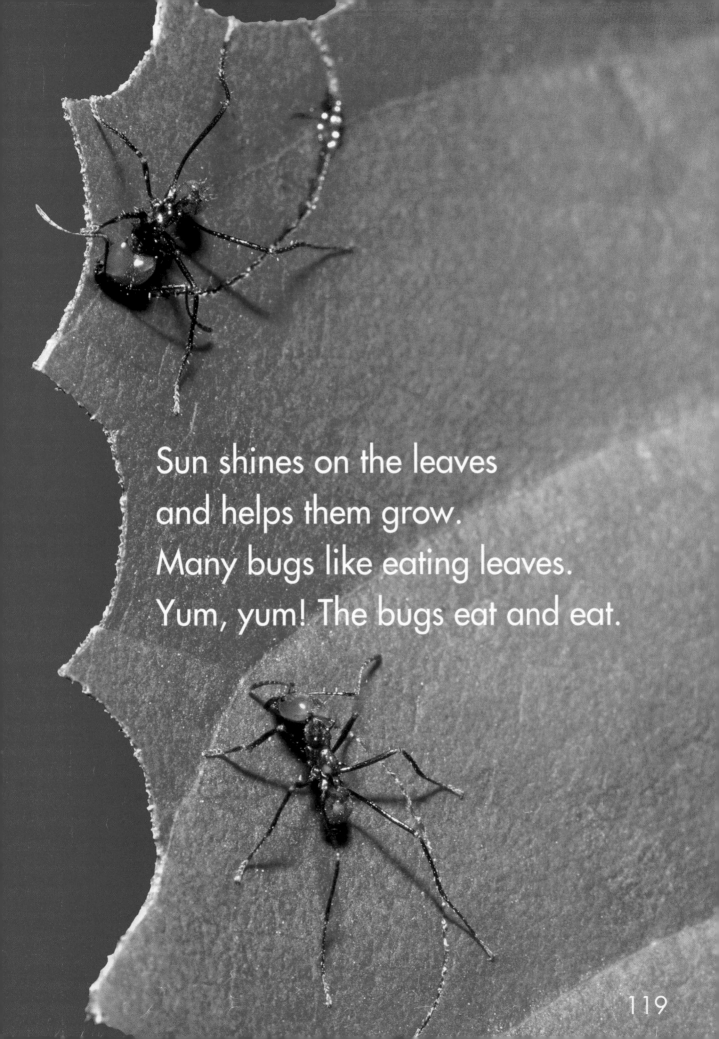

Sun shines on the leaves
and helps them grow.
Many bugs like eating leaves.
Yum, yum! The bugs eat and eat.

A woodpecker sits on a branch.
Peck! Peck! Peck!
The woodpecker pecks for bugs.

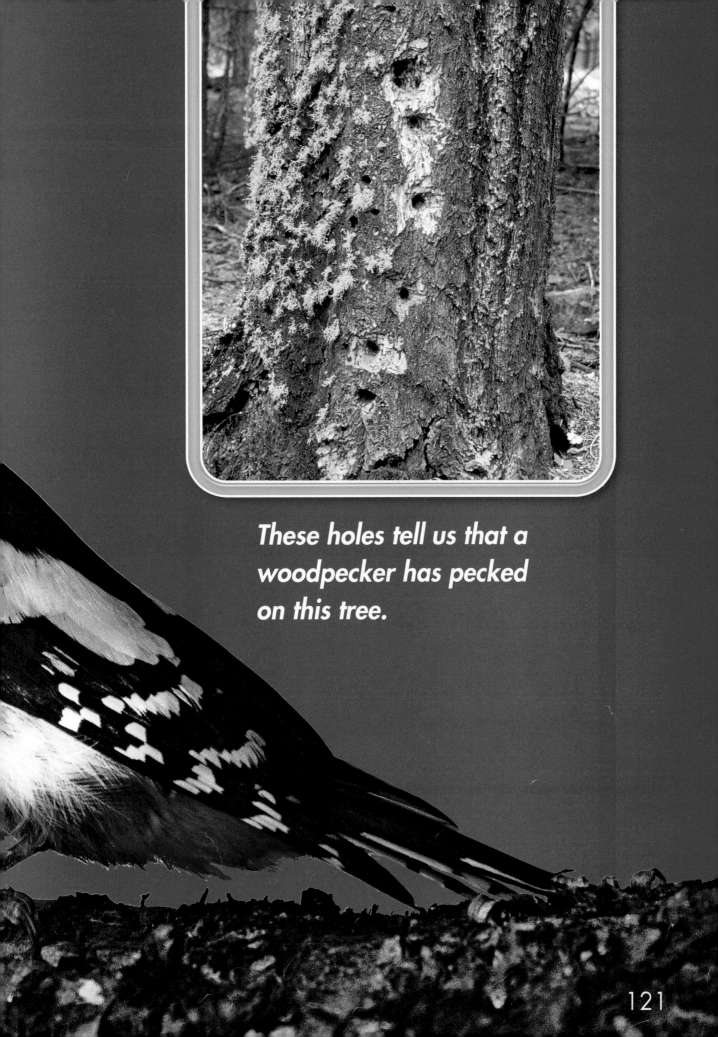

These holes tell us that a woodpecker has pecked on this tree.

This huge log is soft and damp.
Water has made the log rot.
Small bugs made a home in the log.

This bird hops on the log
and pecks at it. Yum, yum!
It gets bugs from the log.

Nuts grow on trees and then fall all around. Squirrels find the nuts and eat them.

*A fox is cute, but it likes to catch small animals like squirrels.*

The black bear eats leaves, grass, and nuts. It likes grubs too. Grubs are small bugs under rocks and logs.

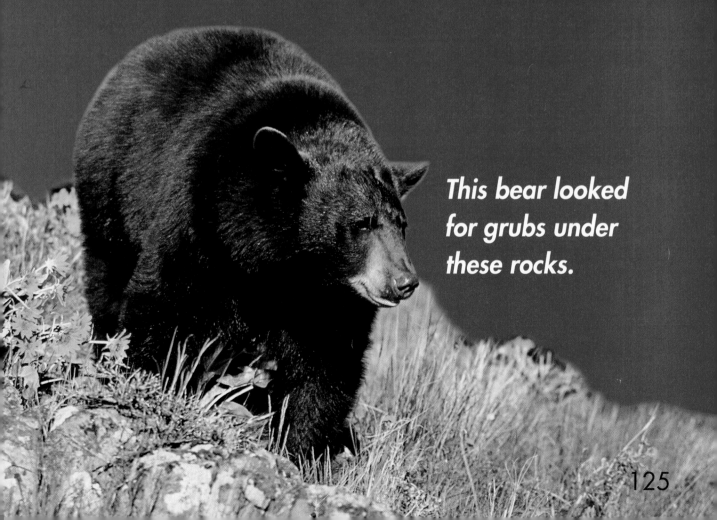

*This bear looked for grubs under these rocks.*

*A hummingbird uses its bill to get food from this plant.*

Many plants have shapes like tubes. Small hummingbirds like to sip food and water from these plants.

Hummingbirds can catch bugs
for food too.

The forest is filled with life.
Many animals and plants call it home.
It is a busy place!

# Think and Share

**Talk About It** Tell what you learned about the forest that you didn't know before.

1. Use the pictures below to summarize what you learned about life in the forest.

2. Why do you think the author wrote *Life in the Forest?*

3. What did you do to get ready to read *Life in the Forest?* How did that help you?

**Test Practice**

**Look Back and Write** Look back at pages 124–125. What do the squirrel and the fox eat?

**Meet the Author**

# Claire Daniel

Claire Daniel learned about forests on a three-month hiking trip with her husband. "That was an amazing experience—being in the forest and living in it."

A bear came to their campsite once. "We heard him coming, so we ran to a shelter. It was a frightening experience! The bear went into our tent and then backed out of it, not finding any food."

**Read more books by Claire Daniel.**

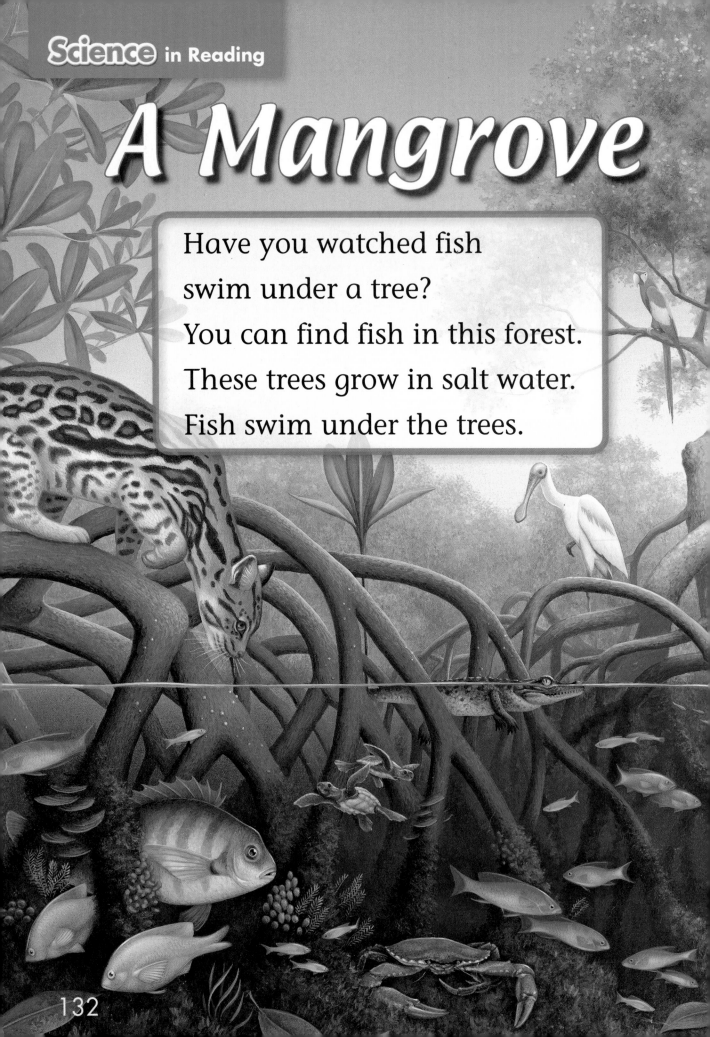

# A Mangrove

Have you watched fish
swim under a tree?

You can find fish in this forest.

These trees grow in salt water.

Fish swim under the trees.

# Forest

*by Terry Lynk*
*illustrated by Russell Farrell*

Lots of animals live here.

Some live in the water.

Some live out of the water.

They are all around this forest.

133

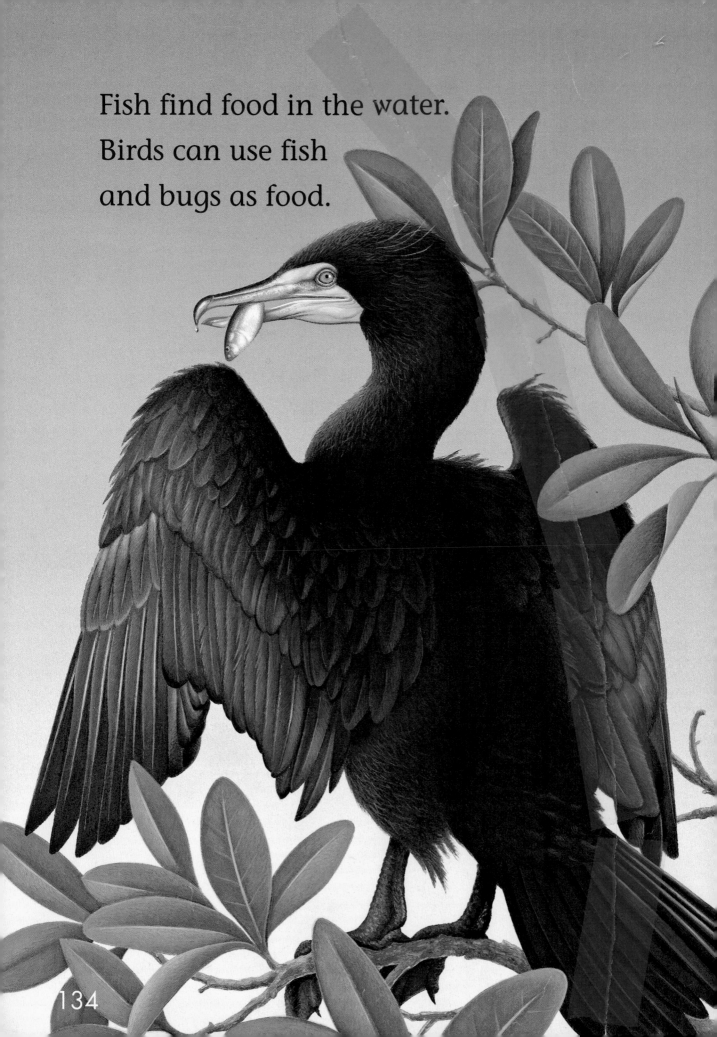

Fish find food in the water.
Birds can use fish
and bugs as food.

But some forests like this
are being lost. We must
save these forests.

# One and More Than One

Many nouns add **-s** to mean more than one.

 **nut + s = nuts**

**bug + s = bugs**

This bear looked for **grubs** under these **rocks.**

The bear is looking for more than one grub. It is looking under more than one rock.

136

# Write Using One and More Than One

**1.** Pick three forest animals from *Life in the Forest.* Write the words that name them. Then write the words again to show more than one.

- - - - - - - - - - - - - - - - - - - - - - - - - - - -

**2.** Write a sentence telling what squirrels eat. Use **-s** to show more than one.

- - - - - - - - - - - - - - - - - - - - - - - - - - - -

**3.** How do woodpeckers get their food? Write about what they eat and how they get it. Use **-s** to show more than one.

# Let's Talk About
# Communities
# in Nature

# Words to Read

| family |
|--------|
| other |
| also |
| their |
| some |
| new |

# Read the Words

1. The queen bee rules the bee family.

2. Other bees also live in the hive.

3. These bees do their jobs well.

4. Some bees will make a new hive.

**Genre: Expository Nonfiction**

Expository nonfiction tells facts about real people, places, or animals. This article tells about honey bees.

Honey Bees

# Honey Bees

by Jesús Cervantes

illustrated by Tom Leonard

What happens
inside a bee hive?

The sun shines. The honey bees wake up. It is time for these insects to work.

Buzz,
buzz,
buzz.

In the hive, bees live together
like a family. In the family, there
is a queen bee, many worker
bees, and some drones.

This is the <u>queen</u> <u>bee</u>.
<u>She</u> rules the hive.

These are the drones.
They help the <u>queen</u>.

Their hive is hidden in a tree.
Worker bees keep this hive safe.

It is not good to make bees mad!
Bees will attack.

Worker bees make wax cells in the hive. These wax cells are small holes.

Bees save honey in some wax cells. Little bees live and grow in other cells.

Honey is food for bees. Worker bees feed honey to other bees in the hive. Bees make honey from nectar.

Bees get nectar from flowers.
Honey bees find flowers with sweet
nectar. They take this sweet nectar
back inside their hive.

Worker bees also get
pollen from flowers.

Worker bees feed pollen to
the queen bee and the little bees.
It helps them grow big.

When those little bees get big,
it is time for a new hive.

Worker bees make the new hive.
A new queen will also go with them.

When it gets cold, the bees
will go inside their hive to
sleep and rest. The bees will
wake up when the sun shines.

# Think and Share

**Talk About It** Worker bees are very busy. What do you think is their most important job? Read the part that tells about it.

1. Use the pictures below to tell what you learned about honey bees.

2. How are a queen bee and a worker bee alike? How are they different?

3. What question did you have about bees before reading? How did that help you?

**Look Back and Write** What kinds of bees live in a hive? Look back at page 146.

# Jesús Cervantes

Jesús Cervantes grew up on a lemon and avocado ranch in southern California. He says, "The ranch had lots of bees. They were brought in to pollinate the trees. I wasn't afraid of bees when I was growing up."

Mr. Cervantes thinks bees are great. He says, "I love honey when it's still on the comb."

**Read more about bees.**

# The Ants Go Marching

The ants go marching one by one,
**Hurrah, hurrah.**
The ants go marching one by one,
**Hurrah, hurrah.**
The ants go marching one by one,
The little one stops to have some fun.

And they all go marching down,
To the ground,
To get out
Of the rain.
**BOOM! BOOM! BOOM! BOOM!**

illustrated by Norman Gorbaty

161

Read Together

# Nouns in Sentences

A **noun** names a person, place, animal, or thing. A noun can be in more than one place in a sentence.

Their **hive** is hidden in a **tree.**

Both **hive** and **tree** are nouns. **Hive** is in the naming part of the sentence. **Tree** is in the action part of the sentence.

162

# **Write** Using Nouns in Sentences

**1.** Write this sentence. Circle all of the nouns.

The bees will feed the queen.

. . . . . . . . . . . . . . . . . . . . . . . . . . . . . . .

**2.** Write a sentence that tells what bees get from flowers. Circle the nouns in your sentence.

. . . . . . . . . . . . . . . . . . . . . . . . . . . . . . .

**3.** How does the queen bee get her food? Write about it. Circle the nouns you use.

## Thanks for the Help

connect to
**WRITING**

In this unit, you read about many different communities. Think of people in your community who help you every day. Write a thank-you letter to one of these people. Draw a picture of this person.

Dear Mail Carrier,
Thank you for bringing me letters. You do a good job.

Your pal,
Matt

## Flower Power

The hummingbirds in *Life in the Forest* and the bees in *Honey Bees* both need flowers. Draw a picture that shows how bees and hummingbirds use flowers. Then write a caption that tells about your picture.

## Make a Chart

You have read six stories about communities. Which did you like best? Which did your classmates like? Take a vote. Make a chart with the story titles. Mark a line to show each vote. Give the story with the most votes a star.

| Stories | Votes |
|---|---|
| A Big Fish for Max | /// |
| The Farmer in the Hat | /// |
| Who Works Here? | /\ |
| ☆ The Big Circle | //// |
| Life in the Forest | // |
| Honey Bees | /// |

165

# Pictionary

## My Family

mom
mama
mother
mommy

dad
papa
father
daddy

sister
daughter

This is me!

These are my relatives.

son
brother

uncle     cousin     aunt

baby

grandma
grandmother

grandpa
grandfather

# Pictionary

## My School

chalkboard

map

chalk

teacher

books

computer

ruler

eraser

pencil

scissors

clock

flag

bulletin board

student

crayon

table

chair

lunchbox

school

playground

cafeteria

classroom

169

# Pictionary

**houseboat**

**pueblo**

**log cabin**

**mobile home**

**high-rise**

**house**

**apartment building**

**townhouse**

170

# Pictionary

## Where Animals Live

**anthill**

**nest**

**hive**

**cave**

**den**

**log**

**barn**

**burrow**

**ocean**

**lodge**

# Pictionary

## My Town

school

grocery store

bus driver

post office

crossing guard

STOP

mail carrier

garbage collector

School

# Tested Words

## Max and Ruby: A Big Fish for Max

catch
good
no
put
want

## Who Works Here?

live
out
people
who
work

## The Farmer in the Hat

be
could
horse
old
paper

## The Big Circle

down
inside
now
there
together

## Life in the Forest

around
find
food
grow
under
water

## Honey Bees

also
family
new
other
some
their

175

# Acknowledgments

## Illustrations

**Cover:** Daniel Moreton
**8, 164** Mark Buehner
**11-35** Jody Wheeler
**38** Pat Cummings
**68-77** Tim Spransy
**74-75** April Mosakowski Hartmann
**78-102** Richard Bernal
**132-135** Russell Farrell
**138** Amy Vangsgard
**142-157** Tom Leonard
**144** Norman Gorbaty
**172** Stephen Lewis

## Photographs

Every effort has been made to secure permission and provide appropriate credit for photographic material. The publisher deeply regrets any omission and pledges to correct errors called to its attention in subsequent editions.

Unless otherwise acknowledged, all photographs are the property of Scott Foresman, a division of Pearson Education.

Photo locators denoted as follows: Top (T), Center (C), Bottom (B), Left (L), Right (R), Background (Bkgd).

**9** ©Bill Ross/Corbis
**10** ©Gabe Palmer/Corbis
**11** (T) ©Tom & Dee Ann McCarthy/Corbis, (BL) ©Sean Justice/Getty Images, (CR) ©Britt Erlanson/Getty Images
**36** ©Ariel Skelley/Corbis
**37** (TL) ©LWA-Dann Tardif/Corbis, (BL) ©Tom & Dee Ann McCarthy/Corbis, (TR) ©Gabe Palmer/Corbis
**57,** 58 Wagner Farm, Glenview Park District, Glenview, IL.
**60** (CR, CL) ©G K & Vikki Hart/Getty Images
**61** ©Melanie Acevedo/FoodPix
**64** Getty Images
**65** (T) ©Patrick Ward/Corbis, (BL) ©Michael Newman/PhotoEdit
**84** ©Stephen Wilkes/Getty Images
**85** (T) ©Paul Souders/Getty Images, (BL) ©Stephen Frink/Corbis
**113** ©Royalty-Free/Corbis
**114** ©Naturfoto Honal/Corbis
**115** ©Steve Kaufman/Corbis
**116** ©Bill Ross/Corbis

**117** (TR) Photowood Inc./Corbis, (TL) Steve Kaufman/Corbis, (CL, BR) ©Royalty-Free/Corbis
**118** (C) ©Photowood Inc./Corbis, (BL) ©Tom Uhlman/Visuals Unlimited
**119** ©Steve Kaufman/Corbis
**120** ©Naturfoto Honal/Corbis
**121** ©Fritz Polking/Visuals Unlimited
**122** ©Jamie Harron/Papilio/Corbis
**124** ©Stephen Dalton/Photo Researchers, Inc.
**125** (TR) ©Gerard Fuehrer/Visuals Unlimited, (B) Getty Images
**126** (T) ©Jim Clare/Nature Picture Library
**127** (T) ©Frederick D. Atwood
**128** (Bkgd) ©Bill Ross/Corbis, (BR) ©Royalty-Free/Corbis, (TR) ©Melissa Farlow/Aurora & Quanta Productions, (CL) ©Gary W. Carter/Corbis, (TL) ©Bill Dyer/Photo Researchers, Inc.
**129** (TL) ©Stephen Krasemann/Getty Images, (BR) ©Tim Thompson/Corbis
**131** ©John Kreis Photography
**135** ©Theo Allofs/Danita Delimont, Agent
**136** Getty Images
**137** ©Stephen Dalton/Photo Researchers, Inc.
**138** (BC) ©Ewing Galloway/Index Stock Imagery, (CR) ©Tim Laman/NGS Image Collection
**139** (TL) ©Karen Moskowitz/Getty Images, (CC) © Colombini Medeiros, Fabio/Animals Animals/Earth Scenes
**168** ©Tim Ridley/DK Images
**169** (CR) ©Richard Orton/Index Stock Imagery, (BCR) ©Mary Kate Denny/PhotoEdit, (TR) ©David R. Frazier/Photolibrary, Inc./Alamy Images, (BR) ©Ed Bock/Corbis
**170** (TL) ©Jan Butchofsky-Houser/Corbis, (TR) ©E. R. Degginger/Color-Pic, Inc., (BCL) ©Royalty-Free/Corbis, (CC) ©Richard Bickel/Corbis, (BC) ©Kim Sayer/Corbis, (TCL) ©Tony Perrottet/Omni Photo Communications, (BL) Getty Images, (BR) ©John Coletti/DK Images
**171** (BR) ©Steve Shott/DK Images, (BL) ©Douglas Peebles/Corbis, (TR) ©Karen Moskowitz/Getty Images, (BC) ©Roger Leo/Index Stock Imagery, (CC) ©Stouffer Productions/Animals Animals/Earth Scenes, (TC) ©Frank Greenaway/Courtesy of the National Prey Centre, Cloucestershire/DK Images, (BCL, TL, CL) Getty Images, (CR) ©Fritz Polking/Visuals Unlimited, (TR) ©Frank Greenaway/DK Images

## Glossary

The contents of this glossary have been adapted from *First Dictionary.* Copyright ©2000, Pearson Education, Inc.